SHOPT

BOW

PAUL HANNON

HILLSIDE PUBLICATIONS
20 Wheathead Crescent
Keighley
West Yorkshire
BD22 6LX

First Published 2009

© Paul Hannon 2009

ISBN 978 1 870141 91 8

The sketch maps are based on 1947 OS one-inch maps and earlier OS six-inch maps

Cover illustration: Parlick from Beacon Fell
Back cover: Slaidburn
Page 1: River Brock, Brock Bottom
(Paul Hannon/Hillslides Picture Library)

Printed by Steffprint
Unit 5, Keighley Industrial Park
Royd Ings Avenue
Keighley
West Yorkshire
BD21 4DZ

CONTENTS

INTRODUCTION

The Forest of Bowland Area of Outstanding Natural Beauty sits within North Lancashire, overlapping into North Yorkshire, and is bounded by Lancaster, Settle, Clitheroe, Longridge and Garstang. Bowland's two faces are the dome of rugged moorland and the softer valley country found largely in the south-east of the region. Linking them is the chief river of Bowland, the sparkling Hodder, supported by Lunesdale and Wenningdale to the north, Wyresdale to the west and the Vale of Chipping to the south. Though seemingly isolated, Bowland borders the Yorkshire Dales and Fylde Coast, and is highly accessible to the Lancashire conurbations and indeed West Yorkshire. Nevertheless, it boasts solitude and wildlife in abundance. Bowland became a royal forest in 1332 for the purposes of deer hunting, and was soon a part of the Duchy of Lancaster, as much still is today. Much of the land is in fact held by vast estates, and the moors are highly prized grouse-shooting country.

Chipping

The majority of walks are on rights of way with no access restrictions, or established access areas and paths. A handful also take advantage of 'Right to Roam'. Existing access areas and concession paths now largely fall within these vast swathes of Open Country, and on most days of the year you are free to walk responsibly over these wonderful landscapes. Of various restrictions, two most notable are that dogs are normally banned from grouse moors; and also that the areas can be closed to walkers for up to 28 days each year, subject to advance notice. Most likely times will be from the start of the grouse-shooting season on August 12th. Information can be obtained from the Countryside Agency and information centres.

Though public transport within the area is limited, bus services strike into most villages: rail stations are also found around the perimeter. Whilst the route description should be sufficient to guide you around, a map is strongly recommended for greater information: at the 1;25,000 scale the Ordnance Survey's Explorer OL41 covers all the walks.

USEFUL INFORMATION

·Lancashire Countryside Service (01772-534709)
·Bowland Visitor Centre, Beacon Fell (01995-640557)
·Bentham Tourist Information (015242-62549)
·Clitheroe Tourist Information (01200-425566)
·Garstang Tourist Information (01995-602125)
·Lancaster Tourist Information (01524-32878)
·Preston Tourist Information (01772-253731)
·Settle Tourist Information (01729-825192)
·Open Access (0845-100 3298)
·The Ramblers (020-7339 8500)
·Traveline - public transport information (0870-608 2608)

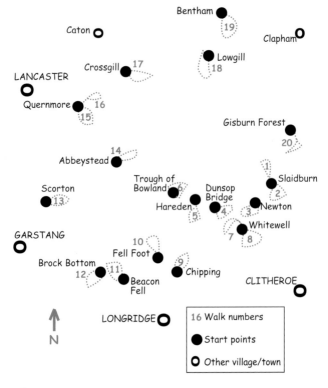

BOWLAND

20 Short Scenic Walks

Bentham
19

Caton

Clapham

Lowgill
18

Crossgill   17

LANCASTER

Quernmore   16
15

Gisburn Forest
20

Abbeystead   14

Trough of
Bowland 6
Dunsop
Bridge   Slaidburn
1
2
Hareden   5   4   3   Newton
Whitewell
Scorton   13
7   8

GARSTANG

10
Fell Foot   9
Brock Bottom   11   Chipping
12   Beacon   CLITHEROE
Fell

LONGRIDGE

16 Walk numbers
● Start points
○ Other village/town

↑
N

6

A RECORD OF YOUR WALKS

WALK	DATE	NOTES
1		
2		
3		
4		
5		
6		
7		
8		
9		
10		
11		
12		
13		
14		
15		
16		
17		
18		
19		
20		

*4¹4 miles
from Slaidburn*

**An unassuming but charming
circuit of Croasdale Brook
by delightful field paths
with extensive views**

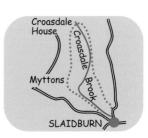

*Start Village centre (GR: 713523), car park
Map OS Explorer OL41, Forest of Bowland & Ribblesdale*

To many still part of Yorkshire's West Riding, Slaidburn remains the capital of Bowland, as it has been since the days of the hunting forest. The Hark to Bounty pub was home to the forest courts, and the panelled courtroom is preserved. St Andrew's church dates from the 15th century: adjacent is the lovely old grammar school of 1717 that survives as the village school. There is a Post office/shop, tearooms, heritage centre and youth hostel, while the arched bridge on the Hodder overlooks a spacious green. Leave by the side road along the front of the pub, and climbing away past the health centre take a good path into the wood on the right. It traces Croasdale Brook through trees to a stile at the end. Advancing a short way with the brook, the path then slants up to a stile into a field. Heading away with the hedge, a moorland skyline appears ahead. Crossing a driveway keep on to a stile at the end. A thin path advances on with the brook again to a wall-stile at the end. Over a slab bridge on a sidestream, cross the field centre to a gate up to the right. Rise away with a wall, swinging right with it at the top on a short, enclosed green way leading to Myttons Farm Crafts.

From a stile left of the house bear right over the field to a corner stile. Joining a track go right over the bridge to derelict Bridge End, and take a small gate to its left. Rise above the stream to a stile by a barn, then cross a long pasture to a stile at the end. You emerge with big views to the long moorland skyline on your left around to Croasdale Fell ahead. Cross the field to a gate/stile, then over a gentle brow to the far corner, with a stile just to the right of a driveway. A trod contours right across the sloping pasture under the renovated house at Simfield, to a hurdle-stile beneath it. A short enclosed path leads past the garden edge to a tiny footbridge into trees. A path drops straight down the wooded bank to a kissing-gate at the bottom, then across to a wooden footbridge. Croasdale Brook is finally crossed at this, the walk's turning point.

Joining Croasdale House drive turn right, away from the farm and on past some barns. After crossing a tiny stream leave the drive and cross to a stile near the brook. Continue downstream towards Shay House Farm, emerging via a stile onto its drive at a bridge. Don't cross, but from a stile opposite resume downstream. As the brook curves away right, keep straight on to a ladder-stile in the wall ahead. Head away with a meandering stream to the far end to briefly meet the brook again, and up to a wall-stile in the corner above. Across a track rise up the field with the stunted remains of a line of hawthorns. Halt here to look back on a glorious scene to the fells enclosing Croasdale. A wall-stile is met on the very brow, after which a straight line uses stiles to pass through several fields on this slight dome. Approaching a line of trees bear left to a corner-stile. Go straight through and Slaidburn appears ahead. Descend towards it, locating a stile onto the road just short of the bridge over Croasdale Brook, which is re-crossed to finish.

Croasdale Brook above Slaidburn

*3¹₂ miles
from Slaidburn*

**A brief ascent gives wide
views before an easy
descent to the bank of
the delectable Hodder**

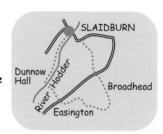

*Start Village centre (GR: 713523), car park
Map OS Explorer OL41, Forest of Bowland & Ribblesdale*

For a note on Slaidburn see page 8. Leave by crossing the
bridge and climb to the steep bend. Fifty yards beyond, a gate on
the right sends an inviting fieldpath slanting away. Already there
are big views back over the village to the wall of fells beyond.
Approaching a wall, bear left with it on a good path running to a
stile at the far end. Advance on the continuing wallside past a
plantation. The brow reveals a fuller prospect of Easington Fell
ahead, and just beyond the end of the trees take a gate in the wall
to resume on its other side. After a short descent to a road, cross
straight over to follow the drive down to Broadhead Farm.

Pass left of the main buildings and round the back to
cross a farm bridge on Easington Brook. Entering a small fenced
enclosure, bear right to a gate into a field and cross to one in a
fence just ahead. Bear right up the large, domed field, diagonally
away to the far corner, with Skelshaw Brook to the right. In the
corner is a tiny footbridge, but don't use it: instead, take a gate on
the right and cross a small stream, going on to Skelshaw Brook just
beyond. Neat stepping-stones supplement the ford, then rise to a
small gate in a fence just above. Bear left up the fieldside outside
the wooded brook, curving up the edge to a gate onto the access
track at the massive house at Skelshaw. Turn right on the access
road to commence a long, simple descent to the valley at Easington.
This gives ample time to appraise an extensive panorama as the

vast eastern slopes of Totridge, Beatrix, Dunsop and Croasdale Fells rise beyond the Hodder Valley. At the bottom the driveway bridges Easington Brook and runs pleasantly downstream with it to a fork. Branch right to the imposing Manor House, passing through the farmyard and out onto a narrow road.

Go left a few steps to a gate opposite. Head directly away with a fence, soon crossing it at an old iron kissing-gate. The big house in view across the river is the austere Victorian pile of Dunnow Hall. Turn right down the field centre, aiming left of the trees to find an iron kissing-gate hidden in a dip. Beneath it is an old iron footbridge, from where cross to the broad river bridge on the Hodder just ahead. Across, ignore the track heading away towards the hall, and turn right on a permissive path upstream in glorious surrounds. The grassy bank of the Hodder is a delight, even allowing for the interruption of a sewage works where the path is deflected around three sides of it. An impressive limestone scar thrusts out of the wooded bank above, while Slaidburn church soon appears. Back with the river, its bank is traced all the way back to the village. Note the distinctive strip lynchets, ancient cultivation terraces, across two fields over to the left. The way merges with a path from the church as it runs through trees to enter the green.

The Hark to Bounty, Slaidburn

11

*3¼ miles
from Newton*

**Some beautiful riverside
walking and big open views
compensate for one
less-endearing quagmire**

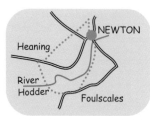

Start Village centre (GR: 697504), car park
Map OS Explorer OL41, Forest of Bowland & Ribblesdale

Newton-in-Bowland is a lovely stone village overlooking the sparkling Hodder. Across from the late Georgian Parkers Arms is the equally attractive hall, while other delightful old buildings overlook luxuriant greens. Leave by descending to Newton Bridge on the Hodder, and across it take a kissing-gate on the right. Head down-river, not quite on the bank as you pass a fence corner to find a stile at the end. The path then runs atop a grassy bank to join the river fully. This is a grand spot backed by the moorland wall of Totridge. After a short while, through another stile the river turns away, and here bear left up an obvious line to a gate/stile in the fence ahead. Continue slanting left to a gate and then on towards a converted barn that appears ahead at Foulscales. In the hedge to its left is a stile onto a road.

Turn briefly right to two barns, then right again along a broad parkland driveway. Remain on this for a quarter mile until a stile on the right. Cross to another then through marshy ground to a suspension footbridge. Cross the Hodder in exhilarating fashion, then bear left up the field to the base of a wooded knoll. Pass through a stile, past a limestone quarry eaten into the knoll, and on to a footbridge on a stream. From this cross to a stile onto a road.

Go briefly right just as far as a stile on the left. Cross the field into a corner in the trees ahead, meeting an old drive with a gate/stile just across. Head away, with a pond at the isolated house of Heaning over the hedge to your left. At the end cross the drive to a stile in the corner, then ascend a tilted bog (aargh!) to dry ground above. Continue rising with a line of trees to a wall-stile in a kink. Just above is the brow, big views featuring Totridge, Hodder Bank Fell and Easington Fell, with Beatrix Fell and Burn Fell just to your left. Advance to a gap-stile just right of the corner, marked by a massive standing stone. Continue on the wallside to a stile at the end which deposits you onto a back road. For a direct finish turn right down this lane, passing on the brow the Quaker burial ground, while lower down is the old Friends' Meeting House: dating from the 1760s, it only ceased its role in 1988.

From a stile opposite head away to drop down to a tiny stream. Behind, pass through a narrowing into another field, but bear right on a part sunken way to a stile just ahead. Entering newly planted trees head directly away, soon reaching the edge from where continue alongside the trees. A path of sorts runs down to cross a small stream, then on to a gate/stile at the corner. Leaving the trees ignore the stile in front, and double sharply back right down the inviting sloping pasture to re-cross the previous stream just above a confluence. Continue on this line, through two gateways and a grassy way forms to reach a gate/stile at the end. Advance to a gate into a garden just ahead, passing left of the house and then going left on the driveway down onto the road in the village.

Newton-in-Bowland

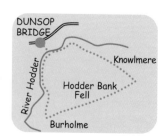

*4¼ miles
from Dunsop Bridge*

**A low fell with excellent
views is sandwiched
between the banks of
the lovely River Hodder**

Start Village centre (GR: 660500), car park
Map OS Explorer OL41, Forest of Bowland & Ribblesdale

Dunsop Bridge claims to mark the centre of Great Britain
and 401 associated islands - see the phone box. By the riverside
green are St George's church, Post office/shop/tearoom and WC.
Leave the eastern end of the village past the car park, then take a
drive on the right to bridge the Hodder at Thorneyholme Hall. On
your right is a lovely watersmeet as it absorbs the River Dunsop.
Immediately across, take a small gate on the left from where a
good path is squeezed tightly between riverbank and wall. At the
wall end emerge and take a small gate on the right into a field.

Bear left, steadily away from the river to a fence corner,
then follow the fence along to a stile ahead, with a tree-lined
stream behind. Now bear right up to the far corner of the pasture,
and at a junction of ways pass through a gate/stile in the wall to
join a grassy track. Turn left on this wallside path, a grand stride
along to a gate/stile where the wall drops away. The track goes
straight on, rising through a part messy corner then along through
lovely surrounds to a gate/stile alongside a house at Mossthwaite.
Pass through and out past another house on the driveway. This runs
on for some time, passing Victorian Knowlmere Manor and along
through parkland to stone-arched Giddy Bridge on Birkett Brook.

Don't cross, but leave the driveway by doubling steeply
back right up the grassy bank to a stile above, at a distinct ditch.
Rise again to a stile above, then slant right up the pasture to a stile

14

in the fence part way up, well short of the barn at Matril Laithe. Rise more directly again now to a gate in the skyline wall above, between plantations. This accesses the open spaces of Hodder Bank Fell, and a good path rises through tussocks. Quickly gaining the brow, a stone post marks the high point at about 656ft/200m. Looking back, Penyghent joins Fountains Fell on the Dales skyline.

Occasionally moist, the path runs grandly on before dropping gently to a corner of the fell. From the stile in this wall corner a fine path escapes a moist corner and heads away, dropping through bracken by a fence on the edge of Fielding Clough. This remains a grand descent with views over the valley to the limestone skyline of Long Knots. At the bottom a stile finally crosses the fence: drop down the field bottom to a stile just above the stream, then down again the short way to a footbridge at Burholme Farm. Don't use it but take the track right, fading but crossing a couple of fields to gain the Hodder with Langden Holme Farm just across. Upstream, a rough pasture is entered via an old iron gate. The watersmeet of Langden Brook and the river is passed, with Langden Bridge seen beyond. Passing an iron aqueduct, continue along your bank through a couple more stiles before a tree-lined pasture leads to a farm drive at Thorneyholme. The path is ushered round the outside to the bridge where you began.

River Hodder below Dunsop Bridge, looking to Totridge

*4¾ miles
from Hareden*

**A steep but memorable
climb to a landmark fell,
with a rougher descent
to a lonely valley**

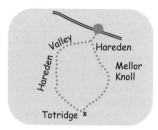

Start Hareden (GR: 643506), on the Trough road
1½ miles west of Dunsop Bridge, roadside parking
Map OS Explorer OL41, Forest of Bowland & Ribblesdale
Access Open Access area, see page 5: spring descents to
Hareden Brook best avoided to protect ground nesting birds

From the road turn down the drive bridging Langden
Brook and follow it to the farming hamlet of Hareden. Cross the
bridge on Hareden Brook to run by the front of the farmhouse
(1656 datestone), then over another bridge before an attractive
cottage. Leave the track by a stile on the left to ascend a field,
pausing to look back over this sequestered scene. Bear left to a
gate/stile at the top corner to meet a track skirting the outside of
a plantation before fading. Climb half-right up the steep, expansive
pasture, eventually meeting a wall near the top. Going left with it a
green track forms to approach the top corner. Up to the right is
Totridge's seamed face. Before the top, however, close in on the wall
so as not to miss the gate/stile from where a concession path sets
off (150 yards before top corner). Now entering a vast, sloping
rough pasture, curve round beneath the top wall to the far corner.
A fence takes over to ascend to a stile at the top onto
open fell. Continue the steep climb, now with a wall again as a thin
path forms on delectable turf. A splendid prospect looks over Hareden
Farm backed by rolling moorland spurs. Higher, as the wall angles
left, continue straight up the path to suddenly meet an inviting
grassy rake. This stunning old path slants left then right through

16

bilberries to fade at the edge of the climb. A thinner path now takes up the running, rising gently left onto the heathery moortop. As this fades it runs onto the broad ridge ahead, at which point swing left for the final minutes: the OS column soon appears, and a thin trod can be found leading past a tiny pool to gain the trig point. At 1627ft/496m Totridge is one of the great Bowland fells. On view are its neighbours Parlick, Fair Snape Fell, Ward's Stone, Wolfhole Crag and White Hill; further north is shapely Penyghent.

Next objective is the valley of Hareden Brook, unseen to the west. So, without a path for the next half-hour, simply head down the opposite side of the fell to the one you ascended. Through heather and occasional peat the descent gently begins, and you will quickly see a shooters' track zigzagging up past a cabin on the flank of Hareden Fell opposite. It matters little as to where you gain the valley, but aim right of the zigzags to meet the track on the valley floor. Grass gradually replaces heather, as you pick your spot to cross the brook to join the firm track. Should you encounter a fenced enclosure lower down, simply deflect to its right.

Once on the track, all that remains is to follow it down-stream through this attractive valley. Another cabin stands below the track, which after a little kink drops onto the flats to shadow the lively brook. This highly enjoyable conclusion runs to a foot-bridge and ford at the limit of Open Country. Remain on the track (concession path) as it runs by water intakes to a house, where it becomes surfaced to lead back out through Hareden onto the road.

Totridge

17

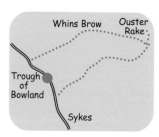

*3$\frac{1}{2}$ miles from the
Trough of Bowland*

**An easy moorland tramp
through open country
at the very heart
of Bowland**

*Start Sniddle Holes (GR: 626527), parking area at foot
of steep drop from road summit a mile north of Langden
Map OS Explorer OL41, Forest of Bowland & Ribblesdale
Access Open Access area, see page 5*

Head east on the road down from the pass, becoming
enclosed to reach Trough Barn. Amid steep fellsides, this side valley
through the Trough of Bowland is known as Losterdale, its stream
a tinkling delight. Through the stile at the barn a firm track climbs
above a wooded bank, outside a plantation before easing out to run
to the top end of a small wood. Through the gate are the remains
of Trough House, beyond which the track rises right with a wall.
Ahead is a broad amphitheatre below the skyline horseshoe of
Whins Brow and Staple Oak Fell. Curving uphill the track passes
through a gate in the wall, and runs between a small wood and a wall,
briefly, before opening into rougher terrain. As the wall drops away
a little further, a thinner path takes over. This maintains a clear
slant up through reeds to a bridle-gate in a wall. Entering Open
Country a grand little path climbs the moor alongside a ravine to
quickly gain the level ground of the moor-top.

Joining a fence from the right, the path runs to a fence
junction. This marks the summit of the bridleway, to which you will
return after a short detour to appraise the Brennand Valley from
above. Through the bridle-gate head on through moister, heathery
terrain, quickly swinging left to find the ground suddenly falling
away. The Ouster Rake path here commences an enjoyable descent,

but all you need do is find a heathery couch just off the path and savour the moment. Revealed at your feet is the Brennand Valley: Brennand Farm is directly below, its few green pastures couched in a moorland bowl running from Ward's Stone to Wolfhole Crag.

Return to the boundary fence, pass through and turn right up the fence-side. This gentle rise soon eases out to reveal the Ordnance Survey column on Whins Brow ahead. At 1561ft/476m this is the walk's summit, a lonely spot from which to appraise a sweeping Bowland scene. While Totridge rises back across the Trough, eyes are drawn westwards to the Ward's Stone skyline above upper Wyre Country: beyond is the Fylde Coast. Resume with the fence dropping gently away to a fence junction, where remain with the left-hand one to descend gently on good, dry moor-grass. A trod partly shadows the fence, and towards the bottom a minor tussocky spell sees a fence comes in from the left. Cross this to reveal, just a minute further, the summit of the Trough road below, and a steeper final minute puts you onto the road. On the crest at 968ft/295m stands the historic Grey Stone of Trough marking the true Yorkshire-Lancashire boundary. It was through the Trough that the Pendle Witches were transported to Lancaster Assizes. Finish by turning left to make the short, relatively steep drop back to the start, possibly concluding on grass by the tiny stream.

Brennand Valley from Ouster Rake

*4¼ miles
from Whitewell*

**Easy rambling linking a
string of old Bowland
farmsteads high above
the Whitewell Gorge**

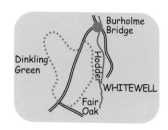

Start **Burholme Bridge, a mile north of Whitewell
(GR: 657479), roadside parking on west side**
Map **OS Explorer OL41, Forest of Bowland & Ribblesdale**

From the junction on the west of the bridge take the
left branch for some three-quarters of a mile, rising pleasantly
past a drive on the right, then entering trees to cross a sidestream:
don't follow, but take a gate to the right and ascend the extensive
pasture with a fence over to the left. Big views up the Hodder
Valley reveal the Dales mountains Penyghent and Fountains Fell far
beyond the fells above Dunsop Bridge. When the fence turns off,
a sunken way forms, swinging right to a gate. It slants gently away
from it to join a farm road, noting a quarry gouged from the hill.
Turn right between distinctive limestone knolls and on to a fork
above Higher Fence Wood. Drop left to the farm, through the yard
and out on a track dropping to Dinkling Green Brook. Across the
footbridge remain in this slim enclosure, dropping left with the
brook. Near the end take a stile in the fence and cross to a gate
just ahead, then descend a field to Dinkling Green. A small gate to
the right of a modern barn puts you into the yard of this historic
settlement with its array of old barns. Turn left on the drive out.

Passing over the brook and then a cattle-grid, look
back to see the splendid 17th century Eshenoke House. The drive curves
round under Long Knots, looking across to a moorland wall from Fair
Oak Fell to Totridge, while ahead is Longridge Fell. Remain on the
drive which curves round again to emerge at a junction by a phone
box. Advance straight on only as far as Higher Greystoneley drive

on the right. Don't take it but use a stile on the left, then bear right to a cluster of barns at Fair Oak. Pass round the right side of the large stone barn: known as the Gunnary, it has a 1729 datestone and a range of slit windows. Through the yard, a junction of ways is reached at the centre. Turn left on a drive past the house, but before the second house turn right down a rough track. The upper house has mullioned windows and a 1716 inscribed tablet. The track drops to a gate and then runs on a fieldside directly away, with the limestone knoll of New Laund Hill ahead and the Whitewell Gorge down to the right. At the end take a stile on the right and follow the curving fence away, reaching a stile in the limestone wall ahead.

A faint path heads away, the broader option crossing a shoulder of the high knoll while a thinner path contours right. Either way, savour a super revelation of Hodder Country at its finest. Behind, the gorge ushers the river through rich woodland, while the fine prospect up-dale embraces sweeping uplands from Totridge to Hodder Bank Fell. Part way down the other side pass through a gate in a fence, and by a fence corner beneath an old quarry a track forms to descend to the farmyard at New Laund. Hidden in nearby woods is the cave of Fairy Holes, which has revealed animal bones and an Early Bronze Age urn. Turn left on the drive out, past a 19th century cheese press. At the road on which you began, turn right to finish.

The Gunnary, Fair Oak Farm

*3³⁄₄ miles
from Whitewell*

**Outstanding Hodder Valley
views dominate this ramble
through fields above
the Whitewell Gorge**

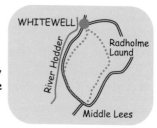

*Start Village centre (GR: 659468), roadside parking
Map OS Explorer OL41, Forest of Bowland & Ribblesdale*

Cheek by jowl at Whitewell are pub and church - indeed there is not a great deal else, but it's a charming spot. The little church of St Michael dates from 1818, while the Inn at Whitewell is an old fashioned country hotel: this was the former manor house, and incorporated in the present building are parts dating back 500 years. Leave by the minor road climbing from the green bound for Clitheroe, past the small social hall. Just beyond a driveway turn up steps to a gate, from which a path rises to a house. Turn right in front of it, and a track passes an aqueduct installation and slants up past a small quarry to the corner of the field. Already you enjoy big views across to Totridge and up-dale to the Dunsop Valley fells.

From the gate at the top, turn right along the wallside to tall iron gates. The way now traces a fence on an easy contour through lush pastures. This stage offers splendid views over wooded Whitewell Gorge to limestone knolls beneath the moorland wall of Fair Oak Fell, while Longridge Fell forms a flat skyline ahead. Past a small quarry with tilted rocks, the fence finally ends at more iron gates. Keep straight on, bearing right to pass through a gate at the far corner and advance a little further to a gate onto a road. Follow this left, gently declining to a junction at Middle Lees.

Noting old roadsigns in the walls either side, go briefly left to the end of the trees. From a stile on the left head away to a sturdy footbridge and turn upstream. Through a stile resume, closing in on the brook rising towards Higher Lees Farm. Towards the top watch for a stile into the brook's wooded environs, then keep straight on to drop to its bank. With dense vegetation on your bank, cross the brook for a few yards only then return to the west bank to rise to the farm just ahead. A stile puts you onto its drive: as this swings away right, go straight on the front of the house and continue along an enclosed track. When this leaves the greenery and turns left, go straight on across the field to a stile/gate ahead. Now bear left up the large sloping pasture, rising above the wood ahead to a stile in a wall-corner. Advance on with the wall enclosing the wood, at the end revealing Radholme Laund just ahead.

Remain with the wall until reaching a corner, then go left with the wall towards the farm. Cross at a gate in it part way along, and resume on the other side to a gate into the yard. Rise straight up and ascend a field with a wall on your right. Reaching a brow, drop to another iron gate combination in the dip, then cross to one to the right. Resume with the wall heading away to a second brow, and start to descend. The walk has saved its finest view, a stunning prospect over the Hodder Valley to a long line of rolling moors. This is a grand finish as you descend through a stile and more steeply, with the hotel visible below. Lower down bear right to a stile in the wall below, then drop more steeply to the house at the start, retracing opening steps down to the road on the hamlet edge.

The Inn at Whitewell

*3¼ miles
from Chipping*

**Easy walking with big
views from gentle slopes
above an archetypal
Bowland village**

Start Village centre (GR: 622432), car parks
Map OS Explorer OL41, Forest of Bowland & Ribblesdale
Access Open Access area (tiny section), see page 5

Chipping is an attractive village whose origins pre-date its emergence as a market town in 1203. Features of interest include pubs, a cafe, Post office and a couple of shops. Worth seeing is a former school, endowed by cloth merchant John Brabin in 1683. It sports mullioned windows, and forms a tidy group along with adjacent almshouses. St Bartholomew's church has 16th century origins: great semi-circular steps from the main street is a novel feature. Wolfen Mill dairy produces quality Lancashire cheeses.

Leave by the side road past the church, and at a junction fork right to descend by a renowned chairmaker's dating from the 1840s. Climb past it to a lovely millpond that once powered it. Part way along turn off at a stile by a drive, and head up the fieldside. Ahead, Parlick thrusts itself forward: looking back, Longridge Fell forms a long skyline over the village, with Pendle Hill further back to its left. Keep straight on at the top, and from a stile at the end advance over a large field, bearing left to the bank above Dobson's Brook. A little further pass beneath a small hollow, and a little path heads off to contour round the bank to a stile part way down. From it the thin path runs on to enter scattered trees, reaching a footbridge on the right arm of a confluence. Climb the field behind to the left of the house at Windy Hills, and turn right into the yard. From the far side of the barn a green track climbs the fieldside.

Through a gate/stile at the top it swings right and peters out, simply remain with the fence on your right through two gates/stiles. A wall takes over, and just before a modest brow, turn off left, crossing to a stile then bearing right to a corner stile onto the head of a surfaced road. Ignore the farm road continuing uphill to Burnslack, and turn sharp right along another track, an old road. On the brow it reveals a good view out to the twosome of Pendle Hill and Longridge Fell, while Burnslack and Fair Oak Fells form a great wall above you. The track enters rough pasture at a gate to ford Leagram Brook, with stepping-stones also here.

Immediately across, take advantage of Open Access and ascend the bank to trace the brook downstream through this rough pasture, all too quickly reaching a bridle-gate in a wall at the end. Leaving Open Country, a bridleway passes through and drops down to a ford below. While you can cross if the water is low, better to take a step-stile on the left to join the driveway of Park Gate in front. Turn right on it out over the cattle-grid and away through fields to a junction with a firmer drive. Go left to pass the farm at Chipping Lawn and continue through the parkland of Leagram Hall to absorb its drive. Follow this down to the road to take advantage of a concession bridleway through the belt of trees on the right, shadowing the road until joining it further along at an attractive lodge. Chipping church tower is a magnet now: arriving at the war memorial, turn right for the village centre.

Leagram Brook

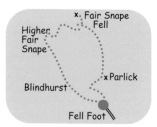

4³4 miles
from Fell Foot

**A truly classic Bowland
fellwalk on the skyline
above Bleasdale;
excellent underfoot**

*Start Cul-de-sac road to Fell Foot (GR: 599444)
north-west of Chipping, roadside parking*
Map OS Explorer OL41, Forest of Bowland & Ribblesdale
Access Open Access area, see page 5

Rise to the house and through a gate onto the open fell. Turn left on a green path along the base, above a wall and through reeds, sheeptrods assisting to approach a fence ascending the fell. Contour round to cross at a hurdle and round again to cross a stream behind. Slant back down the other side on a reedy, sunken way to arrive above a stile. Advance on, shortly leaving the access area at a gate. A green way continues, rising slightly to look down on Blindhurst. A minor brow is reached revealing a super Bleasdale prospect: this features your ascent onto Fair Snape Fell from Higher Fair Snape. Rounding the brow, cross a sunken way ascending from farm to fell, and your own way becomes sunken as it begins to slant right down the flank. Dropping to a firmer track below, cross the stile behind and drop right to another track. Shortly after fording a small stream bear left off the track, slanting down to a stile. Aiming for the farm at Higher Fair Snape ahead, cross the large field to a stand of trees which shelters a footbridge on the tiny River Brock.

Just behind is a stile back into fields. Rise away with a fence and watercourse on your left, crossing at a stile to resume on a grass track up the other side. This runs on fieldsides to a farm road: go right to Higher Fair Snape. The first house has mullioned windows, the second a coat of arms. Just above is a fork of paths:

the right branch is a concession path for Fair Snape Fell. It rises a little then turns right through a gate and beneath modern barns. At the end a fenced track rises into a field, ascending the side to a gate and up to a top one. Winding up another field to a gate onto rougher slopes, it slants right on a delightful rise to a stile onto true fell. Continuing briefly with the wall, it quickly doubles back to commence a zigzag on a brilliantly made way. Effortlessly reaching the top, it peters out just as a faint path is joined. This runs left 150 yards to the west top of Fair Snape Fell at 1673ft/510m. Two cairns and an OS column play second fiddle to a practical stone shelter. The view has now opened out to embrace a distant Lakeland skyline beyond the nearer hills of Three Peaks Country.

Leave by striking south-east for Parlick, a good path crossing a stile to the descending ridge. Bleasdale's fields and farms are encircled far below, with island-like Beacon Fell beyond. At the ridge-wall continue down to the saddle, passing rashes of stones on the slopes where Nick's Chair sits beyond most of them. At stiles and an access notice comes a short pull by the fence to Parlick's 1417ft/432m summit cairn. The panorama features the West Pennine Moors, South Pennines, Longridge Fell, Pendle Hill, Easington Fell and round via Saddle Fell to the Bleasdale moors. Leave by a path heading south-east to quickly encounter steep ground, with Fell Foot directly below. On encountering a traversing path, take advantage of its easy gradients and turn right on one of its sunken ways, thence doubling back to the base of the fell. This not only helps prevent erosion, it makes a more civilised descent.

Parlick from Saddle Fell

*4³4 miles from
Beacon Fell Country Park*

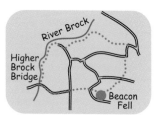

**The wooded banks of the
Brock offer an extended
riverbank ramble from a
colourful miniature fell**

*Start Bowland Visitor Centre (GR: 564426), car park
Map OS Explorer OL41, Forest of Bowland & Ribblesdale*

Beacon Fell boasts 185 acres of moorland and woodland, and its visitor centre has information, shop and cafe. Leave by turning right along the road, clockwise for a few minutes through the trees. At a sharp bend right, a short path goes left through the plantation to a stile into a field giving sweeping views over the Fylde. Descend to a wall-stile, then down a large pasture to a kissing-gate into a new wood. A path drops to a footbridge, and steeply down a wooded bank into a field. Bear left to a corner stile onto a road, right a few yards then down White Lee Lane all the way into woodland to drop to the River Brock at Higher Brock Bridge. Don't cross but turn upstream below a house, Brock Mill. A stile after Brock Mill Cottage puts you into a field which is crossed to cut a bend of the river, rejoining it at a stile in the corner. Enclosed by a fence the path clings to its bank through a lovely stretch, until approaching a marshy area where it turns to climb the bank. Rising to meet a firm track, follow this left. Overlooking an aqueduct, the track drops to an isolated building. To its right a path runs along the foot of a wooded bank. At the end the wooded river gives a grand stroll to Snape Rake footbridge.

Without crossing turn right up the hollowed way, steeply to follow a dead-end road away. At the end of the wood on the left, re-enter on a bridleway that slants back down. As it doubles sharply back left there is a choice of ways: the public path keeps straight on, over a tiny stream to a field corner then along to the end to pick up a track descending from Waddecar scout centre. More popular is the bridleway continuing to the valley floor to turn upstream: it crosses the river at an unclear point, leaving an unofficial path to continue upstream to a big clearing to pick up the scout track. Continuing, a path leaves the track to cling to the river, and the track peters out approaching a stile out of the trees. A faint path continues through a couple of fields to a footbridge spanning the southernmost of the Brock streams at their confluence. Don't cross but turn right past a low ruin to a stile, and a path continues upstream through a landslip in the trees. Quickly finding yourself on a feeder of the main stream, the path runs to a bridge. Across, it slants up the wooded clough to a stile at the top, out into the open. Head directly away, bearing slightly left with a line of old hawthorns, aiming for the cone of Parlick.

Open views see Beacon Fell upstaged by the Bleasdale fells. The old hedge turns away just short of a gate ahead. Follow the fence on your left rising faintly on: at a junction at the end pass through a couple of stiles and turn right along the fence to Wickens Barn. The path diverts left onto a road: turn right, and leave by a drive rising to a house at the top, Heatherway. Use a stile on the right, and within a minute, at a break in the fence, a thin path ascends the large pasture to a stile at the top. It continues up open ground to the road encircling Beacon Fell. Virtually opposite, a forest road slants right through trees. Emerging into daylight at a junction with a bike trail, turn left a short way then take a path rising right through a few trees to a bridle-gate onto open moor. It climbs to a second gate, immediately above which is the OS column crowning Beacon Fell at 872ft/266m. To finish follow the main path into trees, over a cross-paths and down, swinging right at the bottom to the visitor centre.

On Beacon Fell

RIVER BROCK

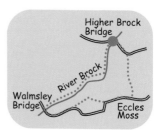

*4 miles
from Brock Mill*

**A charming stroll
alongside and high above
the River Brock on
Bowland's western fringe**

Start **Brock Mill nature trail west of Beacon Fell
(GR: 549430), car park**
Map **OS Explorer OL41, Forest of Bowland & Ribblesdale**

Rejoin the road, cross the bridge and climb steeply away up the wooded bank, completing virtually all the uphill in the first few minutes. On levelling out, advance on to find a stile on the right just past a large house and before a slight dip. Head directly away across the field, soon joined by a fence that was parallel to the left. Above is Beacon Fell's tree-planted dome. The fence leads on to a corner stile, from where cross to one ahead. Continue this line with a fence on your left along the length of a long field to emerge at a gate onto a road at Eccles Moss Farm, with its striking frontage just to the left. Turn right and keep right at the junction, straight on Stannalee Lane. Further architectural interest is passed at Higher Stannalee Cottage with its thatched roof.

Keep on past more isolated dwellings to a sharp bend left at another house, white-walled Rake Head. Just a hundred yards further on the road turn right on the hedgerowed drive to Throstle Nest. On a clear day Blackpool Tower is visible far beyond. At the farm take a stile/gate on the right and advance along a grassy way to the right of the buildings. On your right is the Brock's deep wooded valley. At the end a gate puts you onto a firm track, which leads away to quickly join a minor road. Go right on this hedgerowed, traffic-free way, dropping gently then ultimately steeply down to Walmsley Bridge on the River Brock. The Brock is a little gem, its clear waters draining the amphitheatre of Bleasdale. It is formed by two branches that spring to life on the colourful flanks of Parlick and the fells encircling Bleasdale's remote corner. Only about four miles below Walmsley Bridge it is absorbed into the more substantial River Wyre at St Michael's on Wyre.

Across, take a kissing-gate on the right, and begin your return. A path crosses the field, cutting a corner of the river to join it at a kissing-gate at the end. A brief spell in trees puts you back out into a big open pasture, crossing beneath the wooded bank to rejoin the river at the tapering end. This lovely spell continues through open pastures with the tree-lined river for company, and a complete surround of greenery. Further, a hedgerow comes in to deflect the path left up to a gate onto a track along the base of a wood. Turn right on this to quickly reach a junction at Brock Bottom. A path runs right to the remains of Brock Mill, one of four nearby mills the Brock served: all succumbed to steam-powered mills on the plain below. Continuing past low ruins of millworkers' cottages on the left, another path comes in from a footbridge, which is not crossed. This area has much bluebell cover in season. Resume upstream on the clear path running an infallible, charming and at weekends very popular course back to the start.

By the Brock at Brock Bottom

*3½ miles
from Scorton*

**A miniature fell
and a colourful
little valley: glorious
moorland views**

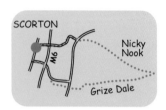

*Start Village centre (GR: 502487), roadside parking
Map OS Explorer OL41, Forest of Bowland & Ribblesdale*

Scorton is a lovely village focused around a large hotel, the Priory. It has a Post office/shop and giftshop/coffee shop. Leave the centre by Snowhill Lane up the side of the hotel, rising past the Roman Catholic church to bridge the motorway. Now a country lane it curves into woodland, passing the drive to the big house of Wyresdale Park. Keep right on the through road, crossing a stream and climbing steeply to a T-junction. Cross the stile ahead from where a path climbs directly up the fell through rampant gorse. This is colourful country: looking back over the plain, observe the Wyreside Lakes, Heysham power station, Lancaster University, the M6 motorway, Blackpool Tower, a wide sweep of Morecambe Bay, and a massive line of the distant Lakeland Fells.

Through a kissing-gate alongside an attractive small reservoir, open country is entered. Advance to the brow, and with a small stand of Scots Pine ahead the path bears right, bound for the waiting Ordnance Survey column on Nicky Nook. The reedy pool of The Tarn below makes a fine foreground to the Ward's Stone skyline. Over a crossroads of ways the path surmounts a broad ridge, passing a large cairn before reaching the trig point. At a modest 705ft/215m this is the summit of the walk. Ahead now is a fine moorland prospect, with the upper reaches of the River Calder burrowing deep into Hawthornthwaite Fell and the Bleasdale moors. A contrasting feature of the 360-degree panorama is the flatness of the Fylde, including Garstang and the motorway: it seems Grize Dale is the only thing you can't see.

The path continues away towards a wall. Ignore the stile and bear right to the wall corner, at once reaching the edge of a steep drop: Grizedale Reservoir shimmers in the wooded bowl of Grize Dale. Nicky Nook's finest hour is especially resplendent in spring or autumn colour. Descend the clear path to a stile onto a solid track. Turn right to commence a splendid tramp along the dale, initially alongside the small reservoir. Grize Dale comes from 'gris' dale meaning valley of the wild pigs. The broad path declines very gently as it runs a glorious course along the valley floor, partly through woodland, and with the stream for company. Enjoy some splendid open views of the fellside, which suggests a far greater stature than its very modest true scale. Ultimately the path runs to a footbridge under a small scar. Don't cross, but from the stile turn sharp right across the field. The path slants up beneath a wooded bank to a kissing-gate onto a back road.

Go right, briefly, and just past the houses at Slean End take a stile in the hedge on the left. Descend the field, bearing right to a corner stile above Wyresdale Cottage. Now slant across towards its drive, a pair of stiles giving access to it as it joins Tithe Barn Lane. Turn down through an attractive cluster of dwellings (Tithebarn Cottage is the old tithe barn) to drop beneath the motorway to a junction with Gubberford Lane. Cross to the footway and turn right into the village, passing the tall-spired church.

Wyresdale Lake from Nicky Nook

*4¹2 miles
from Abbeystead*

**An estate hamlet and an
ancient hamlet are linked
amid the River Wyre's
peaceful upper reaches**

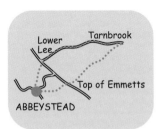

*Start Stoops Bridge (GR: 563543), small parking area
Map OS Explorer OL41, Forest of Bowland & Ribblesdale*

Abbeystead takes its name from an involvement with Furness Abbey. Today it is an architecturally interesting and very private hamlet. A school was founded in 1674: look out also for the pinfold. Some 20,000 acres of grouse moorland are administered from the Duke of Westminster's estate office here. From the charmingly located two-arched bridge on the Tarnbrook Wyre, head along the side road very briefly, then turn left on a track along the edge of trees. This quickly runs to a gate into a field, which is crossed almost to the far end. As you bear right to a foot-bridge, ahead is the enormous house of Abbeystead. Built in 1886 for the Earl of Sefton, its bold front overlooks extensive grounds and is well seen from the path. Just below here the two founders of the Wyre finally merge just prior to its entering Abbeystead Lake, constructed in 1853 to supply mills on the Wyre plains.

Cross the bridge over the Marshaw Wyre and bear left, rising gently across a large pasture well above the stream, looking across to the Abbeystead grounds. As they end, drop left to a footbridge back over the stream. Ascend a steep bank of gorse and scrub to cross to ladder-stiles either side of a driveway. In the next field bear gently right to a path crossroads at a fence corner, finding a stile in a little recess to the right. Follow the fence away on a distinct bank, and through a gate at the end advance to a stile in a hedge in front, just to the right of the farm at Higher Emmetts.

Cross the road and on the short drive to Top of Emmetts. Don't enter, but take a stile on the right and head away with the hedge. From a stile in the very corner briefly follow a fence, then cross a hedge by stiles into a large, reedy pasture. The moorland flanks of Ward's Stone are outspread ahead. Slant diagonally down to a stile in the corner, then pass right of a barn and down the hedge side. Continue along several fields to a short access lane behind Ouzel Thorn Farm. Cross to a stile opposite and over a small field to a wall-stile, overlooking an attractive bend of the Tarnbrook Wyre. Advance along the small enclosure to a gate at the end, then go left on a concrete farm bridge and out along a short walled lane to the road in Tarnbrook. This peaceful old Quaker hamlet was much busier when felt hats and gloves were manufactured here.

Turn left along this narrow access road that runs a pleasant course out from the hamlet, largely with the delightful company of the hitherto moorland stream of the Tarnbrook Wyre. Only towards the end does the stream part company, shortly after which a junction is reached at Lower Lee: Lower Lee House dates from 1694 and was once an inn. Turn right between the buildings and take a small gate on the left, crossing a small footbridge to join a broad track. Bear left on this, a pleasant conclusion as it runs through two pastures, the second having the environs of the Tarnbrook Wyre for company again. The track leads to a wall-stile onto the road just yards from the bridge at the start.

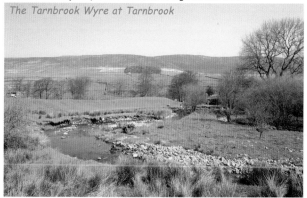
The Tarnbrook Wyre at Tarnbrook

*3¹2 miles
from Quernmore*

**An exhilarating climb
through rugged terrain to
a charismatic Bowland
landmark: stunning views**

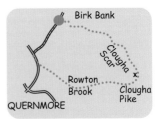

*Start Birk Bank, Rigg Lane (GR: 526604), car park
Map OS Explorer OL41, Forest of Bowland & Ribblesdale
Access Open Access area, see page 5*

A green track rises away from a gate at the back of the car park. Ahead is rocky Birk Bank, still regenerating after long-abandoned quarrying. At a fork bear right then right again, running to a gate. Don't use it but take the path down to the left, using boards to cross a marsh. The path starts to climb the fell, initially through gorse and oak alongside a stream. Rising past the bank of the old quarry the path climbs through rampant bilberries to a wall junction beneath a rocky knoll. From the right-hand stile a wallside path rises away. Within moments it forks on a knoll: take the right branch rising through boulders to slant up the moor. Clougha's upper contours are soon fully revealed above Clougha Scar. The path rejoins the wall to cross it at a small gate, then it improves to rise through a bouldery edge to slowly merge with a higher wall. This is now traced in glorious moorland surrounds, rising only ever steadily. Magnificent views look over the Vale of Quernmore to Morecambe Bay backed by the Lakeland Fells.

The wall falters at the onset of a rocky edge, and a fence branches off left. Pass through a kissing-gate and stile to resume on the main path rising between fence and bouldery edge to a prominent cairn, from where the summit waits just beyond. An Ordnance Survey column at 1355ft/413m shares a platform with sprawling shelters taking advantage of the rash of stones. The fact that a level, heathery hinterland heads away is no real concern on your 'pikeless' pike.: as a viewpoint it adds little to the magnificent scene already enjoyed, save for the inclusion of more moorland, inland to Ward's Stone's great top beyond nearer Grit Fell.

Leave by a much thinner, still clear path contouring away beyond the main shelter, soon bearing right down an inviting groove. Leaving the heather it swings right to cross the grassy moor with an old wall to the right. It drops gently to cross a sidestream and down to a gate in a wall. While the right of way crosses Rowton Brook to remain in Open Country, common usage takes a grassy way down rough pasture to two gates. A trod crosses to the right-hand one, rejoining the moor to descend between wall and stream to a stile out of Open Country. A track descends the field parallel with the brook, crossing it at the bottom to Rooten Brook Farm. Pass between house and barns and down the drive, becoming enclosed at the bottom. After crossing the brook take an enclosed cart track on the right, and beneath a house it descends between walls outside a wood. Emerging into a field at the bottom, drop down to a stile at Old Mill House, secreted in a hollow. Follow its drive out past another house and down onto Rigg Lane. Turn right for two minutes to a junction where Postern Gate Road continues ahead, then bear right on the narrow continuation of Rigg Lane to return to the start.

Clougha Scar, ascending to Clougha Pike

*4¼ miles
from Quernmore*

**Outstandingly colourful
moorland slopes around
the headwaters of
the tiny River Conder**

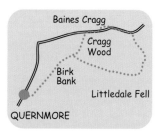

Start Birk Bank, Rigg Lane (GR: 526604), car park
Map OS Explorer OL41, Forest of Bowland & Ribblesdale
Access Open Access area, see page 5

From a gate at the back of the car park follow the track rising away. At an early fork keep left to commence a long, near-level traverse of richly colourful terrain (a robust mix of heather, grass, bilberry, gorse, birch, rocks, scrub) beneath the rocky Birk Bank, still regenerating after quarrying activity. The track runs to Ottergear Bridge, a stone aqueduct high above the stream. It then continues above a birch wooded corner and along the bottom of extensive Littledale Fell to meet a harder shooters' track just above a gate in the wall marking the edge of Open Country: you will return to this point. Turn down the track through the gate, and approaching the house ahead, don't take its drive out but go right over a slab bridge on the tiny River Conder to a stile, from where a little path winds up the scrubby bank to a stile onto a road.

Turn right alongside lovely Cragg Wood, with a fine springtime bluebell display. The road climbs, initially steeply, to reach the open country of Baines Cragg with its vibrant mix of bracken, heather, bilberry, scrub, rocks, brambles and birch. The rocky crest makes a tempting, if unofficial, alternative to the road. On the road, meanwhile, Little Cragg car park is reached just over a cattle-grid. Savour fine views over Morecambe Bay to a skyline from Black Combe through the Lakeland Fells and right round to Great Coum in Yorkshire's Three Peaks Country.

From the car park resume to another cattle-grid with Cragg Farm behind: don't cross it but from a stile on the right a gentle green track slants down to a stile by the right-hand of two gates. Down the wallside the track reforms at a corner to trace the wall down to a gate. The way goes right with a wall along to Skelbow barn. Through a gate to its left a short enclosed way runs to a path junction in front of wooded Sweet Beck. Take the inviting green track rising right to a stile and then along to a ladder-stile into the Open Country of Littledale Fell. Turn right, crossing a marshy trickle followed by the burbling infant Conder to a prominent green way slanting away. Morecambe Bay and the Lakeland Fells are backdrop to a beautiful foreground of Cragg Wood and the Conder Valley.

As the way falters on the moor edge, bear right over adjacent tiny trickles above the heathery edge, and a clear path drops gently to a point where a broader path rises to the edge. This now runs across the moor, becoming a thinner trod running to a point above a prominent group of rocks at an attractive little ravine: the trod runs on past it to join a hard shooters' track just beyond. Turn right as it winds steeply down to a gate/stile in a narrow defile, and down more pleasantly to the gate in the boundary wall used earlier. Don't pass through but turn left on the grassy track to savour the opening mile back to the start.

Morecambe Bay from Littledale Fell

*3¾ miles
from Crossgill*

**Tranquil, wooded surrounds
that will ever after be
remembered as the
bluebell walk (in season!)**

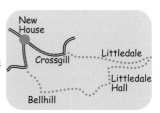

*Start New House Farm (GR: 553625), roadside parking on
Littledale road to east; reached from Brookhouse, Caton
Map OS Explorer OL41, Forest of Bowland & Ribblesdale*

From the junction at the farm turn east on the road to
Littledale, passing through the hamlet of Crossgill. The farmhouse
bears a 1661 datestone: another pleasing house stands before the
drive to Littledale Hall. Just past it is Littledale's former church.
Dating from 1751, St Ann's is now a private dwelling. Beyond it is a
hairpin bend: turn off right through a stile to follow a splendid
green pathway between plantations. At the end keep straight on to
approach a church sat in the middle of a field. This Free Church of
1849 was attached to nearby Littledale Hall: now merely a shell, its
intact stonework and timber ceiling are appreciated by the sheep
that find sanctuary. The evidence of the last ten minutes suggests
The Almighty has fallen from favour in Littledale! At the back is a
solitary grave. The intact one of two slabs marks the resting place
of father and son Dodsons of the hall, the son having beaten his
father here by 39 years. Just beyond, the track forks: the main
one drops down to Littledale Hall, to which you shall shortly return.
For now take the inviting grassy branch up left. Remain
on the field top when the track goes through a gate, and keep on to
a little gate into the top of a wooded bank: a delectable little path
ambles above a bluebell carpet. Emerging at a stile, a grand scene
features Ragill Beck splashing along beneath woodland: your return
route is seen below but for now contour on, crossing a tiny stream
as you traverse the bracken bank. At the end the path winds down

to a sidestream, a nice location for the turning point. Strictly, the path fords the stream to a gateway then turns on the bank behind to drop back down to a stile in the wall. Cross the footbridge and head downstream with Ragill Beck, re-entering woodland at another stile. The bluebell display now truly excels. A stile at the other end precedes arrival back at the arched bridge at Littledale Hall.

Cross to the coach house and turn away from the hall, up through the farmyard. At the last barn at the top, leave by a gate on the right. A grassy track runs upstream with Foxdale Beck - more bluebells! Quickly crossing by a footbridge, a path doubles back to wind up the bank. Leaving the trees at a stile, turn right along the gently rising fenceside. A wall takes over to head towards Field Head Farm. Well before it, take a stile in the wall and pass right of the buildings to gain the drive. Follow this away over a brow (magnificent Lakeland views) and down to Bellhill Farm. Remain on the access road as it swings right, winding down through the fields and along by Udale Beck to emerge onto a back road at Udale Bridge. These charming wooded surrounds of a confluence of becks yield yet more bluebells. Don't cross the bridge but turn right over neighbouring Fostal Bridge, passing a scout camp before a short pull up (vast bluebell carpets on the left) and along to New House.

Springtime in Littledale

3¹₂ miles from Lowgill

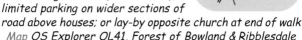

A peaceful ramble around the only hamlet in Hindburn country

Start Village centre (GR: 653647), limited parking on wider sections of road above houses; or lay-by opposite church at end of walk

Map OS Explorer OL41, Forest of Bowland & Ribblesdale

Head up the main street past a tiny green bearing a seat, war memorial and phone box, and up the narrowing up-dale road. With much holly in evidence in the hedgerows, enjoy fine views over the wooded valley enclosed by high moors. Keep straight on at a junction at the houses at Ivah. The road emerges to reach a sharp bend, this section being on the line of a Roman road. Remain on the road as it descends to cross the Hindburn at Stairend Bridge.

Continue a little further to a sharp bend after crossing Mill Beck, and by this confluence take a gate on the right. A track runs through a reedy riverside pasture to cross a stream at the far end beneath a wooded bank. Keep on through a longer pasture to a gate at the end. Here leave the river by bearing left to a gate where a grassy track climbs through an old wall. It rises faintly through colourful country to a ruinous barn. Up to the left is the great bowl of Helks Wood. From a gate beyond the barn, traces of a wall lead across to a notch in bracken slopes, reached via a gate accessing new tree planting. A gate in a line of trees behind sees you up the small bank behind. Advance to cross a deep wooded beck before slanting steeply left to a gate before an old barn. Pass along the front to a gate at the end, then on to a gate above a restored barn.

Cross again to the edge of a deeper wooded stream, then turn down its near side. At the bottom corner a wall-stile admits to Over Houses Great Wood, and a grand little path winds down a dense bluebell bank to approach the river. Through a hurdle-stile at the bottom turn downstream a short way to cross a footbridge on it. This is a gorgeous little spot. Like its neighbour the Roeburn, the Hindburn takes its name from the deer that frequented these parts. Turn downstream to a kissing-gate, and a flight of steps up a wooded bank to a stile. In the field above, a faint grassy track rises to a gate by a barn, then up through a higher field. Instead of going through the gate at the top, opt for a gateway in the hedge to its left, and head along the top of the initially wooded bank to a gate at the far side. The Roman road is crossed again here. The gate admits to Lowgill Lane: go left down to Mill Bridge, a lovely spot. Just across it turn up a narrow lane between buildings, and just above a cobbled hairpin is the drive to Lowgill church.

The stout church of the Good Shepherd features stained glass reflecting its location and name, eminently suited to this isolated farming country. A stile enters a field parallel to the drive, continuing through a gate at the end to a small enclosure next to the churchyard. If visiting the church, a gate in the yard corner accesses this point. This leads to the churchgoers' path from the village. Just behind is the old school: drawing level with it, don't go to the stile at the end, but turn down the steep bank on a partly stepped path to a footbridge in a wooded dell of the Hindburn. Up the other side stay with the right-hand fence, a wall takes over at the top to run to a corner. As a fence takes over turn through the gate and along a part enclosed way to approach the hamlet: the new school is to the right. At new housing, advance to a bridle-gate to the edge of a farmyard then turn right to the road.

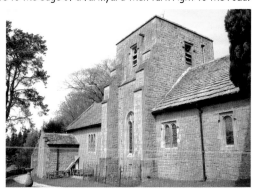

Lowgill
church

*4¹4 miles
from Bentham*

**Grassy moorland and gentle
riverbank play support to
massive Three Peaks views
and a famous landmark**

BENTHAM

Wenning

Forest of Mewith

Lane
Head

Banks

Great Stone
of Fourstones

Start Bentham Bridge
(GR: 667686), roadside parking
Map OS Explorer OL41, Forest of Bowland & Ribblesdale

Bentham (properly High Bentham) is a busy old market town on Bowland's northern limit. Its true colours are shown by being part of Yorkshire: this western outpost of England's premier county is just a dozen miles from Morecambe Bay. Cross the bridge on the Wenning and turn right on a drive. Forking before a caravan park, bear left to houses at Moulterbeck. Pass between buildings to a gate, then left up the field to a stile into trees. A lovely path climbs through narrow confines, past a waterfall before reaching a stile out of the trees. Continue up to a stile at a fence corner, going left on a broad track to the rear of the buildings at Brookhouse.

Through a gate at a ramshackle barn, take another in front and turn right up the field to a stile at the top. Continue to a stile in a tiny section of wall, on to a gate at a fence corner, then on a fenceside to approach Bowker House. An enclosed way leads to the farm buildings, passing to their left and out on the drive. Cross straight over Mewith Lane to a gate just to the left, and climb two fields (intervening stile) to Flannagill on the skyline. From a stile onto its drive, turn along the house front and up to a stile in the garden wall - an alternative runs outside the garden. Entering the grassy moorland of Bents, a gentle rise is made, aided by sheeptrods. The Great Stone of Fourstones appears on the skyline ahead, and two farm drives are crossed en route to it. This intriguing feature was carried here by glacier at the end of the Ice Age. Fourteen hewn steps make its 'ascent' obligatory, its panorama embracing a great sweep of Three Peaks Country dominated by Ingleborough. At 787ft/240m this is in every sense the walk's high point. A path doubles back to information panels on the Slaidburn road.

Follow the road north towards Lane Head, but before the cattle-grid take a short drive right. As it ends cross Burbles Gill by a footbridge, and on the open moor take a thin path slanting left. At the bottom corner leave the moor by a cattle-grid by the house at Holly Tree and follow the drive down to Mewith Lane. Go briefly right and turn down Sunnybank Farm drive on the left. Pass behind the farmhouse into the yard, then from a gate on the left a track slants diagonally down the field to a gate. Through this, turn down the hedgeside to a wall-stile at the bottom. Drop towards the wooded bank below, and bear left along its top to a stone bench overlooking a gorgeous wooded bank falling steeply to the Wenning.

Resume slanting down to a gate, then curve over the tapering field to the farm at Staggarths, with a novel stile into the yard. At the end, don't follow the drive out past the house, but go right through a gate then left across the field to a kissing-gate near the river. Advance on the riverside, around a sharp bend to a gate in a wall. While an unofficial path stays with the river, the right of way goes left along the wall to a stile at the end, then across a large field to rejoin the river at the end. Through a wall-stile, cross to a gateway at a wall/hedge corner, and follow the latter away to a stile onto a back road. Turn right to return to the bridge.

The Great Stone of Fourstones

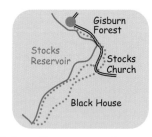

*4¹4 miles
from Gisburn Forest*

**Easy rambling above the
shore of an extensive
lake: binoculars useful
for viewing the birdlife**

Start Water company Gisburn Forest car park
(GR: 732565), off Slaidburn-Tosside road
Map OS Explorer OL41, Forest of Bowland & Ribblesdale

      The near-350 acres Stocks Reservoir was opened in 1932
to supply the Blackpool area, in the process killing off a village and
a way of life. Salt was rubbed into the wound by taking the village's
name: Stocks-in-Bolland was a modest community served by church,
inn, shop and school. During construction work a shanty town grew
up - far larger than anything Stocks had ever mustered - but now
all is gone. Planting began in 1949, and more recently the forest has
improved with more varied habitats and modest visitor facilities.
Gisburn Forest is a centuries-old name for a former hunting ground.
      From the car park return to the road, and on your right
a firm path heads off through the trees. Breaks permit views over
the reservoir before returning you back onto the road at the end.
Turn right over a causeway across a lagoon, then take a firm path
on the left. This runs parallel through the trees then rises away,
swinging right to a fork. Keep right to emerge alongside Dalehead
Church. St James, Stocks-in-Bolland, was built in 1938 as a chapel
where Stocks' souls were re-interred: stones from the old church
were used. At a fork in front of the road drop right onto the road,
and along to the bend by the church. Leave the road by the farm
drive opposite, which gains the brow of Rushton Hill: the reservoir
returns in style backed by a long line of fells, and will be seen more
extensively on your return through the pasture on the right.

The drive drops down to the farm at Black House. Pass through the yard and as it swings left at the end, take a gate on the right. A path rises outside a small wood to a gate at the corner, then merges with a wall on the right. Reaching a plantation corner the path becomes enclosed at a kissing-gate, and runs between wall and fence outside a hard forest track. With open views across to Waddington Fell to the left, remain on this to emerge at the far end, then advance along a fieldside to a gate at the end of the trees. Here turn sharp right over a little brow to reveal the dam just below. Drop left to a stile, then down the edge of new tree plantings onto a firm track just above the grassy embankment of the dam, the walk's turning point. Turn right on the track, and as it shortly swings uphill a more inviting, broad grassy path continues on the tussocky bank. It remains well above the shoreline and beneath a plantation, giving fine views over the broadening lake, with Whelp Stone Crag on the skyline above the vast Gisburn Forest.

When the trees end turn up the plantation side, briefly, then resume across a dip in a large, rolling pasture to contour left to a plantation. A kissing-gate sends a path off through the trees. This soon enters better surrounds as a thoughtfully planted area is crossed to a gate back out. The damper path now runs on above a plantation to quickly emerge via a kissing-gate back onto the road near the church. Turn left to retrace steps to the lagoon embankment, then re-cross it to trace the opening path back to the start.

Stocks Reservoir

HILLSIDE GUIDES... cover much of Northern England

Other colour *Pocket Walks* guides (more in preparation)
·UPPER WHARFEDALE   ·LOWER WHARFEDALE
·MALHAMDALE   ·NIDDERDALE   ·AIRE VALLEY
·BOWLAND   ·HARROGATE & KNARESBOROUGH
·AMBLESIDE & LANGDALE   ·BORROWDALE

Our *Walking Country* range features more great walks...
·WHARFEDALE   ·MALHAMDALE   ·WENSLEYDALE
·HARROGATE & the WHARFE VALLEY   ·SWALEDALE
·RIPON & LOWER WENSLEYDALE   ·NIDDERDALE
·THREE PEAKS   ·HOWGILL FELLS
·TEESDALE   ·EDEN VALLEY   ·ALSTON & ALLENDALE

·NORTH YORK MOORS, SOUTH   ·HOWARDIAN HILLS

·ILKLEY MOOR   ·BRONTE COUNTRY   ·CALDERDALE
·PENDLE & the RIBBLE   ·WEST PENNINE MOORS
·ARNSIDE & SILVERDALE   ·LUNESDALE   ·BOWLAND

·LAKELAND FELLS, SOUTH   ·LAKELAND FELLS, EAST
·LAKELAND FELLS, NORTH   ·LAKELAND FELLS, WEST

Long Distance Walks, including
·COAST TO COAST WALK ·CUMBRIA WAY ·DALES WAY
·LADY ANNE'S WAY   ·NIDDERDALE WAY
·WESTMORLAND WAY   ·FURNESS WAY
·PENDLE WAY   ·BRONTE WAY   ·CALDERDALE WAY

Visit www.hillsidepublications.co.uk
or write for a catalogue